DEVELOPING A TRANSFORMATION AGENDA FOR ZIMBABWE

Shari Eppel, Daniel Ndlela,

Brian Raftopoulos and

Martin Rupiya

2009

This booklet and the roundtable discussions out of which it emerged are part of a project entitled Developing a Transformation Agenda for Zimbabwe, which was a collaboration between Idasa's States in Transition Observatory (SITO) and the Zimbabwe Institute.

SITO States In Transition Observatory
Idasa's Political Governance Programme
www.statesintransition.org

Zimbabwe Institute
www.zimbabweinstitute.org

© Idasa 2009

ISBN 978-1-920118-78-5

First published 2009

Production by media@idasa

Cover by Marco Franzoso

Bound and printed by Logo Print, Cape Town

Note from the publishers

This booklet emerged out of a series of roundtable discussions held in October and November 2008 with stakeholders from all sectors in Zimbabwe and elsewhere in the region, all of whom shared a commitment to tackling the issues that Zimbabwe will face as the interim Unity Government begins to implement policies and attempts to address the challenges of rebuilding Zimbabwe's society and economy. Subsequent events, including further SADC-led negotiations and the swearing in of Morgan Tsvangirai as Prime Minister, have not changed any of the central tenets of these arguments. We have therefore decided to publish this account, with minor editing where necessary to accommodate significant political developments, in the belief that while events have continued to unfold in that country, the observations and recommendations reflected here remain relevant and pertinent, and we hope will help inform the process of reconstruction.

Contents

Pages

Political Crisis, Mediation and the Prospects for Transitional Justice in Zimbabwe

By Shari Eppel and Brian Raftopoulos

Solidarity Peace Trust, Zimbabwe

Introduction

On the 15th September 2008, Zanu PF and the two MDC formations signed a political agreement brokered by Thabo Mbeki under the mandate of the Southern Africa Development Community (SADC).[1] The agreement was the culmination of a process that had begun in March 2007, which was itself preceded by various other attempts by African leaders, as far back as 2004, to end the Zimbabwean political crisis. The central aim of the September agreement was to find a power-sharing arrangement that would reflect the balance of political power in the country after the March 2008 elections, which, together with the abortive presidential run-off election in June 2008, left the issue of the presidential election unresolved.

While the agreement left key areas, such as the allocation of ministerial portfolios, unresolved it did establish a basis for moving the political situation forward. However, one of the major silences in the agreement was around the area of transitional justice. This was not surprising given the fact that Zanu PF, the major perpetrator of human rights offences in the post-colonial period, was not likely to support such a process. Moreover, the MDC for its part, though not without its own problematic history of intra-party violence, neither sought to make this issue a deal breaker in the negotiations, nor had the political muscle to enforce such an inclusion. Thus the September 2008 agreement contained one section that set out to:

> ...give consideration to the setting up of a mechanism to properly advise on what measures might be necessary and practicable to achieve national healing, cohesion and unity in respect of victims of pre and post independence political conflicts.[2]

Moreover, this provision was lodged in the context of a discourse in the Agreement that attempted to combine the demand for dealing with human and civic rights abuses with the need to resolve issues around the redress of historical inequalities. Thus the language sought to encompass both Zanu PF's redistributive demands around the land question and the more political demands for democratisation that have become the hallmark of the MDC and civil society movements in Zimbabwe.[3] It is around such tensions in the political landscape in the country that discussions on transitional justice need to be contextualised.

Within the framework of the broad structural and human rights abuses that were a constitutive part of colonial rule, there have been three major periods of human rights abuses: The War of Liberation (1965-79); the disturbances

in Matabeleland and the Midlands (1980-1988); and the era of violence since 2000.[4] The human rights abuses of the colonial period were generated in the long struggles between the violent structural exclusions of settler colonial ideology and practice, and the often intolerant assertions for unity by a nationalist move- ment that was 'majoritarian without qualification'.[5] In the post-colonial period a combination of the authoritarian legacy of settler rule, the militarist forms of nationalist struggles and the monopolisation of the state by the ruling party bred a new round of human rights abuses that have continued into the present period. Moreover, such abuses have been embraced through the passing of various amnesty laws at the end of each of these periods of state-led violence.

From the period of the 1990s, with the emergence of vibrant civil society struggles around constitutionalism and human rights in Zimbabwe, human rights organisations intensified their efforts to place transitional justice questions on the national political agenda. The report on the disturbances in Matabeleland and the Midlands in the 1980s was arguably the first major call for transitional justice in the independence era, and remains a central reference point for con- tinuing work in this field.[6] Its major recommendations centred on the following areas: national acknowledgement; human rights violators; legal amendments; identification and burial of the remains of missing persons and remains buried in unmarked graves; health; communal reparation; and constitutional safeguards. Many of these recommendations remain pertinent in the contemporary period.

Following this report, released in the late 1990s, an important symposium on 'Civil Society and Justice in Zimbabwe' was held in Johannesburg in August 2003. It brought together many of the key civil society organisations working in this field. This symposium set out several recommendations that sought to deal with human rights abuses in both the colonial and post-1980 periods.[7] Many of these recommendations were then included in the recommendations of a workshop held by the Zimbabwe Human Rights Forum on 9-10th September 2008 in Harare. The Forum called for transitional justice mechanisms that would recognise the following principles: Victim-centred; comprehensive; inclusive; consultative participation of all stakeholders particularly the victims; the establishment of truth; acknowledgement; justice, compensation and reparations; national healing and reconciliation; non-repetition; gender sensitivity; transparency and accountability; and nation-building and re-integration.[8] The Forum also set what it termed 'non-negotiable minimum demands for a transitional justice process.' These included:

- No amnesty for crimes against humanity, torture, rape and other sexual offences, and economic crimes such as corruption;

- No extinguishing of civil claims against the perpetrators or the state;

- Comprehensive reparations for victims of human rights violations;

- No guarantee of job security for those found responsible for gross human rights violations and corruption;

- A credible and independent truth-seeking inquiry into conflicts of the past, which holds perpetrators to account and provides victims the opportunity to tell their stories with a view to promoting national healing;

- Independent monitoring and reform of operations and structures of the police, army, paramilitary, security coordination, administration of justice, food distribution and other organs of state involved in the implementation of the transition;

- Development of interim or transitional rules to guarantee the rule of law and upholding of all basic rights during the transition, including the right to engage in political activities. These rules must be enforceable. They must be encapsulated in amendments to the Constitution or an interim constitution. Such rules must remain in place until free and fair elections are held and until a final Constitution, endorsed by the people, is in place;

- Gender equity in official bodies and for transitional justice initiatives to pay particular attention to marginalised communities in Zimbabwe.[9]

These demands were very much a wish list of desirable processes and outcomes for transitional justice and accord with Alex Boraine's conception of the five key pillars of what he calls a 'holistic approach to transitional justice': accountability; truth recovery; reconciliation; institutional reform; and reparations.[10]

However, it is also clear that such a set of demands are not likely to be implemented, given the nature of the September political agreement in Zimbabwe, and the balance of political power in the country. Thus there is a danger of setting out civic demands for transitional justice that are, to use Mahmood Mamdani's critique of the ethos of the Truth and Reconciliation Commission (TRC) in South Africa, a 'combination of strong moral fervour and weak political analysis.'[11] Moreover, such transitional justice recommendations tend to gloss over the longer term structural injustices that have engendered Mugabe's authoritarian nationalism and the anti-colonial discourse that has constructed the human rights question as a Western imposition. In the context of the failures of neo-liberal economic policies in Africa, the efficacy of transitional justice processes that are not connected to broader structural changes in the economy can very quickly be undermined by revived nationalist politics around redistributive agendas.

It is therefore important to understand the broader global context for the emergence of TRCs in which the latter have 'served as instruments for re-establishing political and institutional stability according to liberal democratic norms' and the discourses of reconciliation, forgiveness and political consensus 'have been understood as the basis for moving forward into an era of market-driven economic progress.'[12] The Zimbabwe crisis and the repudiation of reconciliation politics that accompanied it at the end of the 1990s emerged in the context of a failed economic liberalisation programme.[13] Given the enormity of the current economic collapse in the country and the global catastrophe around de-regulated finance capital in 2008, measures around transitional justice that lose sight of these major structural constraints have little chance of success.

It is the major purpose of this paper firstly, to set out the current political and economic constraints in Zimbabwe and, secondly, to suggest ways in which transitional justice options can begin to be set out. It is hoped that the analysis provided here will present a more realistic assessment of the prospects of transitional justice processes being placed on the national political agenda in Zimbabwe in the current context.

The political context 2008[14]

The elections for parliament, senate, local government and the presidency that took place on 29 March 2008 led to the first electoral defeat for Zanu PF and its president Robert Mugabe. The two formations of the MDC, which split in October 2005, won a majority of 109 seats in parliament against Zanu PF's 97 seats, while the first round of the presidential vote gave the MDC leader 47.9% of the vote compared to Mugabe's 43.2%. The remainder of the vote went to the independent Simba Makoni (formerly Zanu PF). However, the inability of either presidential candidate to win 50% plus one of the votes necessitated a run-off. The state-led violence that preceded this run-off at the end of June 2008 was of such intensity that even Mugabe's long-standing supporters in the SADC and the African Union (AU) could not endorse his election 'victory'.

Mugabe's failure to receive an endorsement in Africa combined with the long-standing condemnation of him from the West added to the pressure for the Mbeki-led SADC mediation to find a political solution to the crisis. On 21 July 2008, both Zanu PF and the two MDCs signed a Memorandum of Understanding (MOU) committing their parties to 'creating a genuine, viable, permanent and sustainable solution to the Zimbabwe situation.' The agreement also set out to achieve the following:

- The immediate cessation of violence and the withdrawal and disbanding of militia groups, paramilitary camps and illegal blocks;

- the normalisation of the political environment;

- the reinstatement of access by humanitarian agencies to the people of Zimbabwe to provide food, medical and other critical services throughout the country;

- the commitment not to take any decisions that would have a bearing on the agenda of the dialogue such as the convening of parliament or the formation of a new government.

On 24 July 2008, Zanu PF and the two MDCs resumed the negotiations that had broken down before the March elections under the mediation of President Mbeki. By 6 August, the negotiators adjourned with several issues outstanding: The duration of the transitional government; the form and structure of the interim constitution; framework issues pertaining to the new government; the powers and duties of the president and the prime minister in the transitional government; and the method and appointment or election of the prime minister and president.

Whereas the South African mediators had crafted a compromise that attempted to spread executive authority of an inclusive government between the president, prime minister and cabinet, the MDC of Morgan Tsvangirai saw the compromise as allowing Mugabe to retain too much power as the head of state. For Tsvangirai and his party, any agreement under the MOU needed to reflect the parliamentary and presidential outcomes of the March elections, effectively installing Tsvangirai as interim head of state until a new presidential election could take place under a constitutional reform process endorsed by a referendum.

In Zanu PF's view Tsvangirai asked too much of the March elections which had left the presidency undecided. The ruling party thus sought to retain as much power as possible under a government of national unity headed by Mugabe, with the Joint Operational Command (JOC), composed of the heads of the army, police and security services, continuing to play a central role. In the words of one of the Zanu PF negotiators, Patrick Chinamasa:

> There is no basis whatever to justify Tsvangirai's demands. He wants President Mugabe to become (former titular President Canaan) Banana. But judging by the March 29 elections there can be no basis for these demands. What he is asking for is a transfer of power, not a sharing of power.[15]

Mugabe's negotiators felt that 'no single party can argue for transfer of power to itself because no single party has the absolute majority to say we are entitled to have power transferred to us.'[16] The growing congruence between the position of the smaller MDC, on the one hand, and Zanu PF and SADC on the other was the result of several factors. These included the increasing tensions and lack of trust between the two MDCs since the 2005 split, the shrinking support base of the Mutambara formation, and the greater reliance on the mediation process by the Mutambara group to secure a foothold in a political settlement. The fact that the minority MDC gained 10 seats in the March election also gave it important leverage with the two major political parties, since it held the votes that could swing the majority in parliament. Since the discussions began under the July MOU, the tensions between the two MDC formations continued. Mugabe was not slow to capitalise on these tensions and attempted to cultivate a closer relationship with the Mutambara group, thus weakening the negotiation position of the opposition.

The result of these tensions between the two MDCs was exemplified in the vote for the speaker of parliament on 25 August 2008. Both MDCs put up rival candidates for the post, with most of the Zanu PF MPs voting for the Mutambara candidate, Paul Themba Nyathi. The Tsvangirai candidate, Lovemore Moyo, won the speakership with additional votes from both Zanu PF and the smaller MDC, dealing a major blow to the smaller MDC. Mugabe was jeered and howled at during his speech in parliament during the election of the Speaker and suffered a deep humiliation. This event evoked a short-term sense of victory. However, the sad irony of watching the two MDCs foreground their own differences before the larger problem of the Mugabe regime spoke to the continuing difficulties of building strong opposition politics in Zimbabwe.

With the ongoing blockages in the mediation process, the MDC (Tsvangirai) adopted a three-pronged strategy against the Mugabe regime. Firstly, it chose to reject the current terms of the agreement crafted through Mbeki's mediation, and to push for the mediation process to be shifted from the SADC to the AU and the United Nations. This position accorded with the MDC's well-known distrust of Mbeki's 'quiet diplomacy,' as well as with the tensions that emerged between

Graeme Williams / South Photographs / africanpictures.net

Mbeki and the EU/US on the Zimbabwe question, with the latter pushing for a UN Security Council decision on sanctions against the Mugabe government. Both the EU and the US repeatedly made it clear that they would only accept an agreement on Zimbabwe that registered a decisive movement of power away from Mugabe. This is the position that the Tsvangirai MDC took in its attempt to move the negotiation initiative away from the SADC.

The second, and perhaps less important, prong of attack by the MDC was to use its control of the legislature to create an alternative centre of power against the executive, blocking attempts by Mugabe to govern outside of a broader agreement. The third part of the MDC approach was a somewhat fatalist belief that the economic crisis would effectively undermine Mugabe's ability to govern.

The first prong of this strategy was unlikely to succeed given that the AU took its cue from the SADC on the Zimbabwe question, particularly since representatives of the AU had been part of the extended reference group attached to the SADC mediation. It would thus be very difficult for the current chairperson of the AU, Tanzanian President Kikwete, who had been critical of Mugabe, to move the AU away from the collective SADC position. With regard to the UN, it was highly unlikely that either China or Russia, particularly in the context of the Georgia debacle, would support another attempt by the West to get a Security Council sanctions vote against Zimbabwe. On the parliamentary strategy, Mugabe had already begun a process, after the March 2008 elections, of whittling down the majority position of the MDC by arresting MDC MPs suspected of engaging in election violence.[17] Such a strategy would more than likely have intensified in the event of a persistent deadlock in the mediation.

Turning to the belief in the capacity of the economy to deal the fatal blow to the Mugabe government, it is clear that the majority of Zimbabweans face the prospect of continued devastation of their livelihoods as a result of the disastrous policies of the incumbent regime. Beyond the profits being made by foreign capital in the extractive sector, and the rent-seeking activities of sections of the ruling elite, the majority of the workforce in both the rural and urban sectors face the likelihood of deepening poverty, if not mass starvation.

Three prominent characteristics stand out in the economic devastation. Firstly, hyperinflation has wiped out the savings and earnings of the workforce in the context of a serious drop in production and major shortages of food, electricity, fuel and all basic goods. As a result, most key transactions in the economy have been dollarised, resulting in rent-seeking activities, speculation, cross-border trading, dependence on remittances from outside the country and criminal activity.

Secondly, there has been a huge decline in formal sector employment and a corresponding growth in the informalisation of labour. The indicators of this process include the shrinking of the formal sector workforce from 1.4 million workers in 1998 to 998 000 in 2004, with the current unavailable data probably indicating further decline; and the share of wages and salaries in gross domestic income dropping from an average of 49% during the pre-structural adjustment 1985-90 to 29% in the period 1997-2003. Moreover, the production crisis resulting from the land occupations has created a double squeeze on the livelihoods of workers as the breakdown of production and incomes in both the agricultural and the manufacturing sectors has placed enormous stress on the reproduction of labour in households.

Thirdly, the economy has witnessed a growing displacement of labour. During the structural adjustment period in the 1990s the volume of urban-rural labour circulation increased because of the difficulties of sustainable livelihoods in the urban areas. This trend has been intensified by the greater displacement of families since 2000 because of the land occupations, electoral violence, the growing diasporisation of the labour force and mass urban evictions during Operation Murambatsvina in 2005.[18] The latter, aimed at clearing away the informal sector in the urban areas and diminishing the opposition's primary constituencies, resulted in the loss of livelihoods of some 700 000 people, and a labour migration process that both pushed numbers of people out of the cities and forced others to find new places in the urban spaces.

While this enormous destruction of the economy eroded the support of the Mugabe regime, the process also presented challenges for the opposition. A central pillar of the MDC since its formation in the late 1990s has been the labour movement. However, this base of opposition politics has been adversely affected by the economic crisis described above, which has in turn created very difficult conditions for political mobilisation in a number of ways. Firstly, the shrinkage of formal sector employment has resulted in a drop in the rate of unionisation and subscriptions, thus undermining the capacity of unions to carry out various organisational and educational activities for their members. Secondly, as a result of this structural decline and more aggressive attacks from the state on union leaders, the labour movement has become more strategically defensive and less able and willing to lead broad civic alliances than it was in the period from the late 1980s to 2000. Thirdly, the strikes and stay-aways that were such an effective weapon against the state in the 1990s when the economy was more buoyant were no longer viable mobilisation strategies in the context of a rapidly shrinking labour force. The informalisation of the labour force has moved workers away from formalised labour practices and protest actions in the public sphere into more individualised and criminalised strategies of survival. The progressive regulation of labour relations that was one of the early achievements of the post-colonial state has been replaced by growing uncertainties around work and formal labour organisation.

This weakening of the labour movement and the culture of worker mobilisation and organisation that was central to it has led to urgent appeals from the once strong Zimbabwean Congress of Trades Unions (ZCTU) for international intervention in the Zimbabwe crisis. A report on a statement made by the President of the ZCTU in 2008 to this effect noted that:

> Mr Matombo said that many of his members are too brutalized by Zimbabwean forces to organize effectively. That is why he will push his group to support stronger international intervention, despite the short-term pain that a blockade or other action could cause to Zimbabwe's poor.[19]

Given the serious weakening of this central organisational base of the MDC it is not surprising that there emerged an almost desperate compulsion to view the economy as an active ally in the struggle against Mugabeism. What amounted to an admission of the diminished capacity of the opposition to mobilise politically at national level was increasingly translated into an adamant assertion of the capacity of an economic crisis to complete the task of that depleted resistance.

Several reports indicated the pervasiveness of this conception. Morgan Tsvangirai was recorded as saying that Zimbabwe's rapid downward economic spiral would 'eventually force Mugabe to compromise,'[20] a view shared by key civic leader Lovemore Madhuku who stated: 'Mugabe will have a difficult time governing without a majority (in parliament), but that is not his real problem. His main and insurmountable problem is the crumbling economy. He has no room to move'.[21] Mugabe himself was aware of this argument and was not slow to link it to his view that this was part of a 'regime change' strategy sponsored by the West. In his opinion, the MDC 'have been promised by the British that sanctions would be more devastating, that our government will collapse in six months' time'.[22]

There was certainly a general opinion, in the opposition and the donor community, that the parlous state of the Zimbabwean economy was unsustainable and that its disastrous deterioration would soon impact on the capacity of Mugabe to continue in office. However, it was also apparent that the crisis was beneficial to key sections of the ruling elite, particularly in Mugabe's major support base, the military. Additionally, there was insufficient information on the survival mechanisms of the poor in Zimbabwe, and the different forms of economic relations emerging out of the crisis, that would allow the economy to persist, albeit at deplorably low levels of survival. Thus to predicate a strategy of change largely on the assumed imperatives of economic decline was to face the danger of underestimating the continued ability of an authoritarian regime to persist.

Political agreement

Given the above analysis it was not surprising that the Mbeki mediation led to a political agreement being signed by the major parties on the 11th September 2008. Mbeki used the limited options available to the major political players at a national level and pressures for change from regional and international forces to push for a political settlement. The agreement that was eventually signed signalled the uneasy relations between a once dominant party forced to concede to the sharing of power and an opposition party unable to muster the pressure to deliver the decisive transfer of that power away from the ruling party. Zanu PF is much weaker as a political party than it was after the 2005 election, while the MDC is not yet strong enough to exert its hegemony over the state.

Amongst the major areas of the agreement are the following:

- Mugabe will continue to be president with two vice presidents from Zanu PF.

- The new position of prime minister will be occupied by opposition leader Morgan Tsvangirai with two deputy prime ministers, one from each formation of the MDC.

- There shall be 31 ministers, with 15 nominated by ZANU PF, 13 by MDC (Tsvangirai) and 3 by MDC (Mutambara), and 15 deputy ministers with 8, 6 and 1 respectively from Zanu PF, MDC (Tsvangirai) and MDC (Mutambara).

- The cabinet will be chaired by Mugabe with Tsvangirai as his deputy and will have the responsibility to 'evaluate and adopt all government policies and the consequential programmes.'

- The prime minister will chair a council of ministers which will oversee 'the formulation of government policies by the cabinet' and 'ensure that the policies so formulated are implemented by the entirety of government.'

- A new constitution will be agreed upon within 18 months as a result of a process that will include the participation of the Zimbabwean public and will culminate in a referendum.

- The implementation of the agreement will be monitored by a Joint Monitoring and Implementation Committee (JOMIC) composed of four senior members from Zanu PF and four from each of the MDC formations.[23]

The agreement left many areas unclear, such as the relation between the authority and decision-making status of the cabinet and the council of ministers, as well as which specific ministries would be allocated to different parties. The latter problem continues to delay the implementation of the agreement as the Mugabe regime persists in its efforts to retain control of key security and economic ministries. However, the agreement should be viewed very much as a terrain of struggle in which both parties will continue their fight for state power in a situation where the ruling party still has the advantage of the control of the means of coercion.

There have been critical positions on the agreement from some key voices in civil society. The Zimbabwe Congress of Trades Unions warned that:

A Government of National Unity is a subversion of our National Constitution and only a Transitional Authority should be put in place with a mandate to take Zimbabwe to fresh, free and fair elections that will hopefully not be disputed by parties.[24]

Moreover, for the chairperson of the National Constitutional Assembly (NCA) the agreement represented a 'capitulation by the MDC.' However it is clear that neither of these social forces have the capacity to resist this process, and indeed the alternative proposed by the chairperson of the NCA of 'going back to the trenches and putting pressure' is, for the moment, more a harking back to past possibilities than a realistic assessment of present challenges.[25] However, other voices in civil society have expressed a more cautious openness to the agreement, willing to explore its capacity to open up political space in the country, while being aware of the lack of political alternatives in the current political conjuncture.

At the time of writing, the agreement signed by the major political formations on the 11th September 2008 is yet to be implemented, halted by a dispute over the distribution of ministerial posts. That the agreement should be mired in such a dispute is a reflection once again that often such struggles over the postcolonial state are viewed as zero-sum battles, with access to the state being the sine qua non for employment, patronage and future accumulation. For the ruling party the danger of losing control of this resource threatens to unravel the rent-seeking structures of profiteering that have become the dominant feature of the fortunes of the political elite. In the case of both MDCs there is clearly a sense that a prolonged period in opposition cannot be sustained in the current context of economic decline. Under these conditions the challenges of introducing transitional justice issues into the political debate will be formidable, and it is this question that the paper attempts to address in the next section.

Transitional justice options in Zimbabwe

This paper began by referring to the demand from civil society in Zimbabwe for an end to impunity, for justice and truth, and for reparations in the wake of many decades of state violence against its own citizens. Both MDCs have stated in their policy documents over the last nine years that a truth commission would be established under an MDC government, and civil society organisations have stated that there should be no amnesties. Interactions at the community level, by ourselves and others, for more than a decade make it clear that many victims urgently desire both justice and the chance to be heard. One of the primary criteria for the likelihood of any formal truth-telling and/or prosecutorial process taking place and succeeding is thus in place in Zimbabwe – namely a strong desire on the part of a significant segment of the population for such a process to take place.[26]

However, there are other important preconditions and realities to be considered in assessing whether a nation is likely to succeed in adopting an official policy of transitional justice. This paper has already located the Zimbabwean transitional justice debate in the context of a near total collapse of the economy, including of health, education and food production, and this collapse is itself indicative of longer-term structural injustices that have enabled Zanu PF to entrench its authoritarianism. Furthermore, any transitional justice process under the current power-sharing arrangement risks being derailed by an ideological clash between the MDC and Zanu PF's understanding of what should be accounted for and whether there should be any accounting at all for post colonial abuses, for example.

There have been at least 25 official truth commissions/commissions of inquiry into human rights abuses worldwide since the June 1974 Commission of Inquiry into the Disappearance of People set up by Idi Amin in Uganda. Most of these have been only marginally successful, or have failed to achieve much – including the 1974 Ugandan one. Among the major challenges facing truth commissions are:

- the problem of 'over-reach' in the context of debilitating economic and political conditions;

- lack of consultation with a broad range of political and civic actors;

- inadequate preparation by groups hoping to make inputs into the process;

- high expectations, particularly around the problems of reparation and prosecutions;

- the absence of long-term institutional follow-up to support the process;

- replicating other country's experiences in different contexts.[27]

Under the power-sharing arrangement, Zanu PF retains control of the Ministry of Justice, the Central Intelligence Organisation (CIO), the army and, because the president appoints the chief of police, will continue to have almost total control of the JOC – now called the National Security Council. It is hard to imagine, therefore, that it will allow prosecutions of, for example, Perence Shiri, now Commander of the Zimbabwe Air Force, who was Commander of the 5 Brigade in 1983/4 when 10 000 Ndebele speakers were massacred in the west of Zimbabwe.[28] Emmerson Mnangagwa, who was head of the CIO in the 1980s and allegedly played a key role in the violence of the JOC during 2008, remains highly influential within the ruling party.[29]

Much of the Zimbabwean bureaucracy has been militarised and military chiefs, found in high places in parastatals and elsewhere, have a vested interest in maintaining the current status quo of impunity to ensure not just their freedom but also their excessive, corruptly gained wealth. Previous reports by human rights organisations have shown clear links between many in senior positions and gross human rights violations.[30]

Furthermore, the impartiality of the courts has been shown to be highly suspect. In this context, how does civil society intend to ensure prosecutions of senior perpetrators? It seems unlikely that Morgan Tsvangirai will push for any process of national accountability at this stage. He has remained vague on the issue of amnesties and prosecutions, and has repeatedly reassured Zanu PF that it would not use its Ministry of Home Affairs (including the police) to seek vengeance.[31] In the interests of preserving the power-sharing deal, the MDC is unlikely to rock the boat by reminding Zanu PF of its transgressions at this stage.

A key criterion for the success of a truth commission is official support at the highest level. If this is missing, the process is likely to be derailed by all sorts

Per-Anders Pettersson / AfriLife / africanpictures.net

of obstacles – for example endless debates around its preparation, a toothless model being agreed to, the suppression of the final report, or creating unacceptable risks to those who come forward to testify.

Zimbabwe already has a very bad record on official commissions of inquiry into human rights abuses since independence in 1980. There have been two formal commissions of inquiry – the Dumbutshena Commission of Inquiry into the Disturbances in Entumbane (Bulawayo) in 1981 and the Chihambakwe Commission of Inquiry into the Disturbances in Matabeleland in 1983 in which about 10 000 people were massacred by the 5 Brigade. It has emerged that at the very time commissioners sat recording statements in February 1984, the same 5 Brigade was actually overseeing further murders in Bhalagwe Camp in Matabeleland South, less than 200km away from where the Inquiry was taking place in Bulawayo. Both of these commissions have had their findings suppressed by the state to cover evidence of state complicity in the abuses. The Legal Resources Foundation (LRF) recently took the government to court demanding the right of the nation to see the Chihambakwe Report. The court ruled in favour of the LRF, but the government then announced that there had been only one copy of the report and it was lost so it was unable to comply.

In short, even though it would not be easy for such blatant suppression of proceedings and findings to occur at this stage in Zimbabwe, we need to be sure that conditions are right for an official, full disclosure of truth before promoting a half-hearted process that aggravates and thwarts the nation's ultimate need for truth and accountability.

Commissioning a commission

Most truth commissions are established by presidential decree.[32] This seems an unlikely prospect in Zimbabwe under Robert Mugabe! The national legislature may create a truth commission, such as in South Africa, but this is less common. Although the MDC has a majority of support in the Lower House, Zanu PF still has the overall legislative power to block such a move in the Senate or to water down the terms of reference and powers of such a commission, possibly rendering it a face-saving but powerless event.

Truth commissions can be introduced as part of a peace accord, but the power-sharing agreement signed by Zanu PF and the MDC in September 2008 does not clearly refer to a formal truth commission, making only a weak reference to 'considering' a mechanism for national healing. This rather tentatively framed clause is a good indication of the ambivalence with which Zanu PF views such a process – it is an agreement to consider such a mechanism, not an agreement to agree to such a mechanism.

The question then remains: should some kind of an official process nonetheless be pushed for at this time? The problem with this is if a commission is instituted and given a weak mandate, or if it turns out that security for victims does not currently exist, the opportunity for a successful outcome will be missed, and it is not likely that a second commission will be set up when the timing is better.[33] Most seriously, testifying before a commission needs to be safe for victims, and as long as Zanu PF remains in control of the army, CIO and the Ministry of Justice, the risk to victims, particularly in rural areas, remains. While it is hoped that Zimbabwe will not deteriorate into widespread violence at this stage, it may be pragmatic to let events unfold over the next year or two and then reassess the degree of official space for a truth commission initiative.[34]

However, while an official truth commission may not be possible or advisable at this time, civil society and the opposition should continue to debate the parameters and mandate of a future truth commission, which may become possible in a year or two. Such discussions, involving all Zimbabweans, could occur in the context of the forthcoming, officially mandated process of debating a new constitution. In terms of the power-sharing agreement, this process will begin with the appointment of the new cabinet and will run for eighteen months.

While official, national transitional justice processes are unlikely to take place, much can still be done to promote 'accountability; truth recovery; reconciliation; institutional reform; and reparations.'

Accountability

Zimbabwean civil society organisations have endeavoured to make the law work for victims of political abuses by prosecuting perpetrators where known. While this has seldom proved successful, on occasion damages have been won through the courts, notably for some of the victims of the food riots of 1998.[35] Civil society organisations have continued since then to attempt to use the law to achieve moments of justice, but this has become increasingly difficult as the impartiality of the judiciary has been undermined, and as the state has turned the tables by passing repressive and unjust laws, which it has then used to criminalise the opposition. The Public Order and Security Act in particular has been used to prevent civic and political activity, with several thousand political arrests since 2000.[36] However, legal records exist of many of these arrests, and using this documentation Zimbabwean lawyers have done a courageous job of trying to insist that the police and the courts hold people accountable, and exposing their failure to do so.

While prosecution of senior government officials is unlikely, the prosecution of many hundreds or even thousands of human rights violators at the community level is more likely – and may well go a long way towards the deeply perceived need for justice currently felt by victims. A very significant feature of the violence of April-June 2008 is that the majority of victims were able to name at least some of their perpetrators; the tragic reality was that it was often neighbours and even family members who were responsible for the horrendous assaults, murders and destruction of property within their own communities.[37]

The result is there have been arrests and prosecutions of individuals who stole cattle from their neighbours or who assaulted them in the context of the political violence. The success of such prosecutions has depended very much on the cooperation of specific local police officers and magistrates,[38] but the precedent has been set. Civil society organisations can continue to pursue such arrests and trials across the country, in both urban and rural settings, by providing free legal and moral support to those willing and brave enough to risk repercussions in the still unstable current context of laying charges. However, prosecution is more difficult in attacks that occurred more than three years ago as the right to claim damages will have been prescribed in terms of current law. An amendment is needed to the law to ensure 'no extinguishing of civil claims against the perpetrators or the state'.[39]

Truth recovery

Civil society in Zimbabwe has already done a remarkable job of keeping track of human rights violations, in particular over the last eight years, but also prior to 2000.

In 1998, the Catholic Commission for Justice and Peace (CCJP) and the LRF released 'Breaking the Silence, Building True Peace: a Report on the Disturbances in Matabeleland and the Midlands 1980 to 1988'. This report, and the processes undertaken to develop it, emulated many of the characteristics of a formal truth commission. More than 1 000 victims of the atrocities came forward to testify to two interviewers over the course of several months, and their testimonies, together with archival evidence, was used to produce a history and a database of abuses. The report included recommendations on what was needed to heal the region. Interest in this report has not waned; it remains the only concerted locally driven effort to document the events of those years. The report was reprinted in 2007, ten years after its initial release, and a summary has also been released in all three official languages.

In the late 1990s, with the food riots in Harare in 1998, the level of state violence rose once more and civil society came together to document and prosecute state offenders where possible. This meant that in 2000, when abuses became widespread ahead of the June election, civil society organisations were ready and able to document them. Since 2000, hundreds of documents and reports have been released by organisations such as the Zimbabwe Human Rights NGO Forum (which releases monthly violence reports) and the Solidarity Peace Trust (which produces two or three major reports a year on violence and related issues). The Crisis in Zimbabwe Coalition, the Zimbabwe Peace Project, Zimbabwe Lawyers for Human Rights, the Media Monitoring Project of Zimbabwe, the Zimbabwe Election Support Network and the CCJP have all produced reports over the last eight years, especially on human rights abuses during election periods. These include thorough medical records of torture, murder and assault, as well as lawyers' records and sworn statements on abuses both in and out of state custody.

In countries such as Guatemala, Brazil, Colombia, Nigeria, Turkey and Morocco civil society groups have led the way in recording the abuses of their governments. In Brazil, while there has never been an official truth commission, the Nunca Mais report of 1985 by church activists and lawyers became a best seller and has achieved something of the status of an official inquiry.[40]

In Guatemala, the Recovery of Historical Memory (REMHI) project produced the Nunca Mas report based on tens of thousands of interviews conducted by the Catholic Church, initiated by their bishops in the wake of the 1996 peace accord.[41] In terms of this peace accord, a Historical Clarification Commission (CEH) was established, but the Church feared that this government-driven process would be highly selective and was not mandated to name perpetrators. They therefore set up a parallel process, and as the Catholic Church reached into the remotest villages in Guatemala they gathered shocking evidence of the massacres and disappearances of 30 000 people.[42] The REMHI report is a remarkable piece of work, running to thousands of pages; a 300-page summary has been translated into 16 languages and sold worldwide. The report, released early in 1999, ultimately fed into and greatly enriched the official CEH report, released later that same year. While the unofficial REMHI report remains more widely read, the combination of these two reports, one official and one unofficial, means that the history of events in Guatemala during the 1980s can never again be denied – and hopefully will not be repeated.

The examples from around the world, and from Zimbabwe itself, show that formal reports can be written and processes that in many ways are identical to official truth commissions, can be undertaken by civic and church groups. Victims can be given the chance to be heard and of having their story recorded, either by individual interviewers or by their local communities, as a result of civic initiatives.[43] If the aim of any truth-telling process is to ensure that the national memory incorporates and acknowledges the suffering of ordinary people during a time of oppression, and records the culpability of the state and the consequences of this for the present and future, then formal but unofficial processes can make a significant contribution. 'Breaking the Silence' managed to do just that, and ensured that the Matabeleland massacres are now very much part of the national memory in Zimbabwe. However, the 'Building True Peace' aspect of this report will rely on the goodwill of a future Zimbabwean government that is prepared to implement the recommendations and other recommendations that may come from future civic initiatives linked to the more recent violations.

As in Guatemala, it is highly possible that formal, detailed reports produced by civil society organisations in Zimbabwe will in due course contribute to an official truth commission process, and also possibly to future prosecutions.

In summary, a truth commission may not be possible or pragmatic in Zimbabwe while the current transitional government is in place, but civil society and opposition groups should continue to debate and consider how a future truth commission should function, and what its mandate should be. Discussion around this issue should not focus exclusively on the post-independence period, but ensure that abuses of the colonial period are also dealt with. This is important not only to historicise properly human rights abuses in Zimbabwe, but also to help ensure a more serious engagement with Zanu PF on the challenge of truth recovery.

International players could play a useful role in providing financial support and building greater credibility for a truth commission. However, the advantages of the involvement of the international community need to be balanced against the

Tsvangirayi Mukwazhi / Independent Contributors / africanpictures.net

dangers of international agendas complicating and stalling a national process.

Extensive consultation around such a process, in particular in rural Zimbabwe, should be undertaken on a continuous basis so that when the time is right for establishing a truth commission, civil society organisations and opposition groups have a good idea of what people expect from it.

Reconciliation

A great deal has been written on how this term should be defined in transitional justice processes, and the concept remains contested. However, most people broadly accept that a major intention of transitional justice is to promote reconciliation at some level, that after massive conflict, relationships between individuals and communities will be damaged and will need interventions to promote healing. It is understood that failure to attempt this could lead to long-term negative repercussions, such as further cycles of violence.

Broadly speaking, reconciliation incorporates peace building, victim empowerment and individual healing, but also needs a context of economic development and extensive social reform. It is hard to imagine that any person or community could begin a real process of reconciling in a nation with 400 million percent inflation, no access to health or education, little formal employment, and with 45% of the country dependent on food donations. A recent pilot survey in Matabeleland in which people were asked to list their communities' priorities found that 100% of respondents rated food as the current most urgent need, followed by water at 87%.[44] The same survey found that most people rated their leadership as either Bad or Very Bad, and rated intra-community relationships as Very Bad, mainly because of the political violence and years of political manipulation of access to resources by local leadership. It is significant that this survey did not interview anyone between the ages of 18 and 25 as this age group was entirely absent in the villages, and women respondents predominated, as a result of the diasporisation of Matabeleland's rural population. Very few able bodied men remain in the rural setting, and this in turn impacts dramatically on the capacity of communities to till land and grow crops – particularly bearing in mind that 9% of these respondents have no donkeys or cows.

We would agree with Brandon Hamber that reconciliation is 'a voluntary act and cannot be imposed'.[45] It is also most difficult for the poorest people in a nation to come to terms with their pasts and to forgive the neighbours who burnt down their homes when they have no prospect of replacing what was lost and face an entirely bleak future. In the face of such extreme poverty, where survival is top priority, what interventions are sensible? We would suggest that peace building and leadership building are needed, but that this needs to occur simultaneously with efforts to economically empower rural families and improve access to basic education and health care. Schools and clinics, where they exist, are barely functioning and have no staff or resources. It will take state intervention and massive interventions by development organisations specialising in small enterprise projects to begin to reverse this situation. It will also require the normalisation of the macro-economic environment so that it becomes financially possible for a teacher or nurse to survive on a formal salary.

We need to begin developing a new culture of leadership that is not about repression and bullying, exclusion and impunity. Many civic organisations in Zimbabwe already undertake conflict resolution programmes, including leadership training and empowerment of ordinary people to challenge leadership. Such organisations need to coordinate their activities and methodologies and expand them to include more grassroots churches, for example. The proposed constitutional consultation process, which is part of the September 2008 agreement, is ideally suited for civic organisations to combine skills training with debate on constitutional issues, including how to hold leadership accountable in the future in Zimbabwe.

Civic organisations and churches in rural communities should discuss local solutions to the recent violence with communities. For example those who destroyed homes could be ordered by local leaders to rebuild homes for their neighbours and make other material reparations at the local level, including of livestock and furniture where possible. There is no need to wait for national consensus on this, but to explore over the next few months where and how this might be adopted by villagers, either through communal court processes under cooperative traditional leaders or through church mediation at local level. Fear and anger remain high in villages affected by recent violence; there is a need for impartial mediation as soon as possible in as many places as possible to prevent further cycles of violence. In Matabeleland, Zanu PF supporters are now afraid and are being ostracised at village level, with some being ejected from village funeral gatherings, for example, and their 'Zanu' maize meal offered at such gatherings being churned into the dust. In a starving community this is an impressive act of contempt and rejection.

In Matabeleland, the issue of mass graves remains important. Once the space allows, it will be a priority to resume the exhumations conducted by Amani Trust Matabeleland in the late 1990s. This is a highly skilled task to be conducted only by properly trained forensic experts, but Amani's experience is that exhumations and the accompanying 'healing of the dead' processes are life-changing tools that lead to conflict resolution and truth telling.

In Mashonaland too, in the wake of the recent violence, there are reports of shallow graves and of bodies being dredged out of dams. These recent disappearances must be dealt with, and a database set up to begin identifying these disappeared. There are well-established databases about disappeared people all over the world, and a request to train interested people in Zimbabwe to access and use such a database has already been activated.

The space exists for many different types of community-based interventions that could contribute to reconciliation. Many transitional justice-oriented activities are already taking place, including conflict resolution and leadership training, and these need to be better resourced and coordinated.

Institutional reform

Institutional reform will need the cooperation of the state. Many of the institutions most in need of reform seem likely to remain in Zanu PF control, yet it is hoped that in a transitional phase, as national polarisation declines, Zanu will be amenable to suggestions on where and how to reform. The police and prison services are in a dire state – characterised by maladministration, politicisation and lack of resources. The justice system barely functions, with massive staff turnover, absenteeism, and empty posts. The magistrate's court in Bulawayo

Graeme Williams / South Photographs / africanpictures.net

cannot find a simple sheet of A4 paper on which to type a letter. There is a need to de-politicise these institutions and to try to reverse the bribery and corruption that predominates in all of them. This will take significant resources, as well as the normalisation of the economy so that police and court officials do not have to rely on bribes and stolen goods for their survival.

Civic organisations can play a key role here in engaging the relevant ministries, documenting the collapse and corruption of state institutions and insisting on a state response. A successful workshop was held in October 2008 in Bulawayo involving senior prison officials and members of civic organisations, including lawyers and former prisoners. There is a need for relevant civic groups in different sectors to undertake more discussions of this nature with officials from state institutions. There is also a need to develop coherent policies and action plans on what can be done to de-politicise the High and Supreme Courts, for example. Training programmes for police and prison officers, magistrates and prosecutors must be developed. This will take decades, but it is possible to strategise around this now. It is not necessary to wait for the state to develop a broad policy to begin developing working relationships with officials that can implement immediate change at the micro level – such as fixing toilets in remand cells and reviving prison programmes to grow food for prisoners' consumption.

Reparations

Most victims of violence in Zimbabwe, whether recent or from the 1980s, will raise the need for compensation. Apart from the desire for justice, the desire for compensation currently rates most highly. However, Zimbabwe has a very poor history of individual compensation, with the War Victims Compensation Fund being looted in the 1990s by those with political connections. In 1997, Mugabe also bent to massive pressure from the War Veterans Association and paid out Z$50 000 per ex-combatant, an act that caused a dramatic decline in the value of the Z$ at that time. Many who did not qualify for benefits received compensation, while genuine victims did not. In Matabeleland, the handful of ex-dissidents from the 1980s who were also ex-ZIPRA combatants received payouts, for example, while those whose lives they had destroyed received no compensation, as this payout was only for ex combatants and not their victims.[46]

Considering the scale of the violence in Matabeleland in the 1980s, and the scale of violence in certain parts of Mashonaland in 2008, there will be entire regions where almost every family may have a legitimate claim to compensation. The question then has to be whether individual compensation is a practical option. In the case of violations that took place a number of years ago families may find it hard to prove their losses at this stage. Furthermore, a system of making people individually responsible for recounting their abuses, especially in a situation of dire poverty, will encourage fraudulent claims and invented histories, and undermine efforts to reach a 'forensic' truth.[47] The expertise and human resources that would be required to check thoroughly every claim would tie up the process for years, resulting in frustration and disillusionment for genuine claimants.

The concept of community compensation should therefore be considered, with individual compensation being restricted to support for families of political murder victims, for example. Individual compensation at the community level could be partly facilitated by perpetrators being forced to help with the rebuilding and restocking of homes that they destroyed. Large, government-driven urban housing initiatives could prioritise those who were displaced by Murambatsvina, and a proactive policy on vending and the informal sector could help those who lost livelihoods to rebuild them without state harassment. Longer-term skills training and possibly small business loans could help shift the informal sector back into the formal sector over time, and all of this could be done in the name of compensation.

Compensation on the scale required will need to be dealt with at the level of government, and probably international donors, but civic groups can consult on community needs and priorities. Communities in Matabeleland, for example, are open to the idea of communal reparation, including improved access to health, education, small enterprises and, in the urban setting, state housing.

Conclusion

There is an overwhelming cry for justice and compensation in Zimbabwe in the wake of the recent violence. It is indeed necessary to put an end to the pattern of 100 years of impunity, but the task is going to be complex, particularly in the current political context. The political space for widespread prosecutions of senior government leaders is not likely to open up at the state level any time soon. It may be highly problematic to push for a truth commission at this stage, as the current transitional government will be too weak and compromised to give such a commission the power that would make its outcomes useful. However, there remain many activities that civic organisations could push for and accomplish; some will require government support and others can go ahead regardless, as long as some level of democratic space exists. Perpetrators could be held accountable at the community level, either through the courts or through a compromise of local reparation. Truth recovery can be ongoing, and civic groups can continue to write reports, although there is a need at this stage to return to source to validate claims made when it was difficult to do so. Peace-building and leadership-building activities that are already taking place need to be expanded and methodologies shared. Civic organisations need to lobby for institutional reform, and to take part in this process where feasible, with training and simple resources. Above all, there is a need for civil society groups to maintain a dialogue with victims and victimised communities, to establish their priorities and understanding of what happened in their area over the years, and what needs to be done about it now. This may vary considerably from village to village, and there should not be an oversimplified approach to what needs to take place at this time.

Recommendations

The battle to place transitional justice issues more squarely on the Zimbabwean political agenda has been going on in one form or another since the 1980s. However, as the country struggles to find a way out of the current political quagmire, and to develop a democratic discourse beyond the stale imperatives of an authoritarian nationalism trapped in the narcissism of its narrow version of the past, the need for a sustainable transitional justice process must be pursued more vigorously. Moreover, the pursuit of the process must be understood as a terrain of competing national agendas within a particular historical and political context that will be one of the key determinants of future political struggles in the country.[48]

As a way forward, this paper recommends the following:

- Accountability: While prosecution of senior government and party officials is unlikely to be possible under the current political conditions, the prosecution of perpetrators at community level is more likely to be accomplished. This can be done both through the court system and through forms of accountability developed through community structures.

- Truth recovery: Civil society groups need to continue with the valuable work of truth recovery that they have carried out since the 1980s. However, this work needs to move beyond the empiricist, forensic nature of evidence gathering to more historical understandings of processes of state and community violence.

- Reconciliation: Processes of reconciliation are more likely to succeed in conditions of economic recovery where the hope of a better future can provide a material basis for linking reconciliation to economic reconstruction. Moreover, at any one time, reconciliation is built around contested notions of legitimacy, and building linkages between different sites of legitimacy will demand careful balancing between the state and different sites of power within society. It will be important, therefore, not to reduce the debate on reconciliation to a moralising voice that places the burden of reconciliation on the victims. A much more sustainable process will link such a debate to material changes in power relations within a society, ensuring growing empowerment for the marginalised and victimised.

• Institutional reform: Indications of reforms within the coercive arms of the state must become immediately apparent in a political transition to begin the long process of building trust in the state. Thus reforms in the judiciary, police and army must begin to point the way towards a greater respect for the rule of law. Once again, a stabilisation of the economy is an essential part of reviving the capacity to deliver in these areas.

• Reparations: In Matabeleland and in some parts of Mashonaland, almost every family would have a legitimate right to claim that they have suffered state-orchestrated human rights violations at some point since the 1960s. However, the problems of how individual reparations should be validated and financed, together with the pressing demands for more general economic recovery and development, mean that communal reparation could be explored as an alternative to individual payouts. There is a need for extensive consultation with victims around any process of reparation.

Acknowledgement

The section in this paper under 'Political Context: 2008' was originally published as 'Elections, Mediation and Deadlock in Zimbabwe?' by the Real Instituto Elcano in Spain. See www.realinstitutoelcano.org/wps/portal/rielcano_eng/Conetn?WCM_GLOBAL_CONTEXT=Elcano_in/Zonas_in/Sub-Saharan+Africa/ARI119-2008

Brian would like to thank the Institute for permission to use this publication.

Endnotes

1   The subsequent implementation of the September 2008 Global Political Agreement was marred by ongoing stalemates in 2008 and required further SADC intervention. At the time of going to press in early 2009, both parties had agreed to move forward with implementation and the interim government had been sworn in to office. Whether or not this

ensures that the outcomes brokered through the agreement are met is an ongoing question. Nevertheless, the central argument of the authors – that the agreement fails to tackle the question of transitional justice – remains relevant, and the unfolding circumstances appear unlikely to change that.

2   Agreement between the Zimbabwe African National Union-Patriotic Front (Zanu-PF) and the two Movements for Democratic Change (MDC) formations on resolving the challenges facing Zimbabwe. 15th September 2008, Harare.

3   For a discussion of the tensions around this debate in Zimbabwe see Brian Raftopoulos, "The Zimbabwean Crisis and the Challenges for the Left." **Journal of Southern African Studies**, Vol 32, No 2, June 2006, pp 203-220.

4   Shari Eppel, 'A Brief History of Violations of Human Rights in Zimbabwe since 1965 to the Present.' Paper prepared for the International Centre for Transitional Justice, New York, October 2003.

5   Terence Ranger, 'Introduction' in Terence Ranger (Ed) **The Historical Dimensions of Democracy and Human Rights in Zimbabwe**, University of Zimbabwe Press, Harare, 2003, p21.

6   The Catholic Commission for Justice and Peace and the Legal Resource Foundation, **Breaking the Silence, Building the Peace: A Report on the Disturbances in Matabeleland and the Midlands 1980 to 1988**. CCJP/LRF Harare, 1997.

7   Themba Lesizwe, **Civil Society and Justice in Zimbabwe: Summary of the Proceedings of a Symposium held in Johannesburg 11-13 August 2003.**, Pretoria, 2004.

8   Zimbabwe Human Rights Forum, minimum demands adopted by participants at the transitional justice workshop, 'Options for Zimbabwe,' held at the Holiday Inn, Harare 9-10 September 2008.

9   Ibid.

10 Alex Boraine, "Transitional Justice: A Holistic Interpretation," in A Boraine and S Valentine (Eds), **Transitional Justice and Human Security**, International Centre for Transitional Justice, Cape Town, 2006.

11 Mahmood Mamdani, 'Reconciliation without Justice.' **Southern African Review of Books**, November/December 1996.

12 Greg Grandin and Thomas Miller Klubock, 'Editors Introduction- Truth Commissions: State Terror, History and Memory,' Special Issue, **Radical History Review**, Issue 97, Winter 2007, p5-6.

13 Brian Raftopoulos and Tyrone Savage (Eds), **Zimbabwe: Injustice and Political Reconciliation**. Institute for Justice and Reconciliation, Cape Town, Weaver Press, Harare, 2004.

14 This section details political developments up until shortly after the signing of the 15 September 2008 agreement. Subsequent events included ongoing disputes about the allocation of ministerial posts and further detention and harassment of MDC leaders and supporters. While Prime Minister Tsvangirai was duly installed, the implementation of the agreement continued to be marred by subsequent interruptions and setbacks, the details of which are beyond the scope of this paper.

15 Jason Moyo and Mandy Rossouw, 'MDC: Brown's Trojan Horse?' **Mail & Guardian**, 22-28 August 2008.

16   Interview of Welshman Ncube, Secretary General of the MDC (Mutambara), www.newz-imbabwe.com/pages/mdc253.18653.html. 22/v111/2008.

17   "Zanu PF 'plots to seize' parliament." **Business Day**, 1st September 2008.

18   'Operation Murambatsvina' is the Shona term for 'clear out the filth', an expression often used by the ruling party to refer to the urban support base of the MDC.

19   Margaret Coker, 'Powerful South African labour group ponders how hard to press Mugabe.' **Wall Street Journal**, 9th July 2008.

20   Basildon Peta, 'Mugabe advised to quit talks.' **Cape Times**, 22nd August 2008.

21   Dumisani Muleya, 'Mugabe to call new cabinet, dealing blow to talks.' **Business Day**, 28th August 2008. This argument is also put forward by Piers Pigou, 'Malice in Blunderland,' **Molotov Cocktail**, 05, September-October 2008. Pigou asserts that 'if Morgan Tsvangirai and the MDC can hold their nerve, the economic pressure on the rulers of Zimbabwe will eventually pay off.' P15.

22   Jason Moyo, 'Mugabe prepares for the next move.' **Mail & Guardian**, 29th August- 4th September 2008.

23   Agreement 15th September 2008 op cit.

24   Statement by the Zimbabwe Congress of Trade Unions, Harare, 16th September 2008.

25   SW Radio Hot Seat Transcript of Interview with Lovemore Madhuku, www.swradioafrica.com/pages/hotseat250908.htm

26   Priscilla Hayner, **Unspeakable truths: confronting state terror and atrocity**; Routledge, 2001.

27   Ibid, page 214. (Also contribution by Priscilla Hayner at an Idasa meeting on 'Transitional Justice Options in Zimbabwe,' Pretoria, 24th October 2008.) The Uganda Commission was set up by Amin as a face-saving measure because of international pressure, but it lacked political commitment to real change. It documented 308 forced disappearances but did not prevent a worse wave of abuses in its wake. Only one copy of the report is alleged to exist in Uganda.

28   CCJP and LRF, op cit.

29   'Exposed: The Mnangagwa, Makoni Plot', **Zimbabwe Times**, 17 July 2008.

30   See Zimbabwe Human Rights NGO Forum reports at www.hrforumzim.com/frames/inside_frame_special.htm. See also Amnesty International, 'Time for Accountability,' November, London, 2008.

31   Most recently at a rally in Harare on Sunday 12 October 2008. Then on 1 Nov in Bulawayo, Tsvangirai called for a truth commission and said that 'without justice we cannot move forward' (Tsvangirai calls for truth commission', AFP, 1 Nov 2008.) This immediately led to Zanu PF accusing Tsvangirai of trying to derail the unity agreement, 'in illustration of the point we are making that a truth commission is too divisive to be successful at this point in time.' (Tsvangirai dabbling in peripheral issues: Zanu PF, www.zimonline.co.za, 4 Nov 2008.)

32   Ibid, page 214, for summary of most common histories of truth commissions in section following.

33   Hayner. Ibid, page 202.

34   At the time of writing human rights violations continue in pockets of the country, notably in Manicaland.

35 The Zimbabwe Human Rights NGO Forum managed to win damages for a handful of victims, but this was challenged by the state. In the meantime inflation has rendered the damages meaningless.

36 See SPT, 'Policing the State,' 2006, for an account of around 2 000 political arrests.

37 Human rights organisations have tracked down the names of perpetrators, but in many instances victims have not been able to name their torturers.

38 SPT, 'Desperately seeking sanity,' July 2008.

39 The Forum, op cit, 10 Sept 2008.

40 Daan Bronkhorst, 'Truth commissions and transitional justice – a short guide for users,' Amnesty International, Netherlands, 2003.

41 Human Rights Office, Archdiocese of Guatemala, 'Guatemala: never again!' Recovery of Historical Memory Project: 1999. Summary published by Orbis Books, Maryknoll, 1999.

42 An estimated 200 000 died in Guatemala during the 1980s under the military rule of Rios Mont, among others.

43 In Bulawayo, the Catholic Church began a process of encouraging victims of abuses to testify in front of congregations in 2002, and these services for justice and peace were then replicated in other parts of Zimbabwe and even in London, where refugees now testify on UN Day in Support of Victims of Torture. The experience of Amani Trust Matabeleland with exhumations also resulted in mini truth telling processes in Matabeleland – see ahead under reconciliation.

44 Masakhaneni Trust: 'A base line report on the means and priorities of targeted communities in Matabeleland North and South,' Bulawayo, October 2008.

45 Brandon Hamber, 'Evaluating projects and programmes for reconciliation and transformation: experiences from the field,' Cape Town conference, April 2007.

46 It must be added that only 122 dissidents surrendered in 1988, but this example serves to illustrate the pitfalls of singling out certain groups for individual monetary compensation and not others.

47 We were recently told by a headman in rural Matabeleland that it should be expected that people would lie about being victims if they thought they stood to gain materially by doing so, as people are so poor. He claimed that when church officials came asking about the post-March violence, some families in his area falsely claimed to have been among those beaten in the belief that these officials were undertaking some sort of 'registration for compensation' exercise when in fact they were simply trying to document what had happened in the area. Personal interview, Lupane, October 2008.

48 For an excellent discussion of the 1979 peace settlement and its aftermath in Zimbabwe see Norma Kriger, **Guerrilla Veterans in Post-War Zimbabwe: Symbolic and Violent Politics 1980-1987**. Cambridge University Press, 2003.

Key Issues for Zimbabwe's Economic Reconstruction

By Daniel B. Ndlela

Zimconsult

Introduction

Setting the context for stabilisation in Zimbabwe

The economic reconstruction of Zimbabwe will need to address the humanitarian crisis that the economic decline has precipitated. This was identified as a priority at the roundtable discussion, initiated by Idasa's States in Transition Observatory (SITO) and the Zimbabwe Institute, held in November in South Africa. This report provides an analysis of the general conditions required for such an action plan, as elaborated by the roundtable discussions, and provides some recommendations for post-election planning and reconstruction of the country's economic sectors. It is hoped that this input will be used in broader consultations with Zimbabwean stakeholders.

The roundtable identified the following critical benchmarks as essential for an environment conducive to Zimbabwe's economic recovery:

- A credible political settlement that is acceptable to all Zimbabwean stakeholders, the African region and the international community;

- Credible first steps that demonstrate commitment to globally acceptable values of political governance (protection of humanitarian rights, sound economic management, commitment to the rule of law, the upholding of human rights and commitment to democratic processes);

- Commitment to a stabilisation package that is acceptable to all non-state stakeholders (business, farmers, trade unions and civil society) as well as the international community;

- Credible institutions with an obligation to carry out the tough mandates associated with an orthodox stabilisation programme, with countervailing measures to be put in place simultaneously to deal with the social costs of stabilisation;

- A credible team of economic managers, starting with the Minister of Finance and Governor of the Reserve Bank of Zimbabwe (RBZ), who can deliver a credible budget and are committed to an internationally supported stabilisation package.

Taking into account the relationship between politics and economics, the roundtable agreed that substantial re-engagement would depend on clear progress in these areas. The credibility of the political settlement will be the primary factor in dictating the parameters and depth of re-engagement, but even with such a go-ahead, engagement will require safeguards to manage the political and financial risks of investing in transition in Zimbabwe. At the political level, the success of Zimbabwe's stabilisation programme will be based on the following benchmarks:

- An economic programme informed by the economic principles adopted by the Global Political Agreement (GPA);

- The establishment of an independent Advisory Council composed of mainly Zimbabwean experts, and assisted by regional and international experts;

- Institutional reform, i.e. the capacity to implement policies that build sustainable broad-based and inclusive growth that, over time, leads to structural transformation of the economy.

Sequencing of the stabilisation programme is as essential as the formulation of the stabilisation programme itself. It is generally understood and accepted that the starting point for a stabilisation programme must be a combination of fiscal and monetary restraint. However, in the case of Zimbabwe, virtually all targets for launching an orthodox stabilisation programme and package are being overtaken by events on a daily basis. There is no single, unique stabilisation model that is applicable to different countries at different times in different regional locations that followed different paths to economic decline and hyperinflation.

In Zimbabwe's case, a central determining fact is the total collapse of the domestic currency as a means of transaction. The country's domestic finance system has virtually been replaced by dollarisation of the economy. Up to the first week of October 2008, there were four legal payment methods: (1) Real Time Gross Settlement (RTGS), (2) inter-account transfers, (3) cheques, and (4) cash. The Central Bank then banned the first two, which were the viable methods of payment. The RTGS was temporarily replaced by a cheque system. In terms of the parallel market rate, this took into account the clearance period or perceived clearance period of a cheque and hence ended up much higher than the RTGS rate. Even with the excessive printing of bank notes, the local printers cannot keep up with the demand created by the government's excessive expenditure.

As a result, Zimbabwe is progressively moving towards de facto (though not yet de jure) dollarisation. Even before the advent of foreign currency shops, it was estimated that over 80% of transactions were already taking place in foreign currencies, mainly the US dollar and the South African Rand (ZAR). The legitimacy of the currency therefore needs to be restored.

Characteristics of successful stabilisation

Stabilisation is a process of bringing down high inflation to moderate levels without major macroeconomic imbalances and at minimum social cost. Experience has shown that approaches such as setting price ceilings for essential goods and interest rates, a fixed exchange rate with exchange controls and wage indexation do not stabilise high inflation. In fact, Zimbabwe has been stuck in this approach without any success since 2002. There is an urgent need to launch a stabilisation programme. The longer the government waits to fight inflation, the higher the social costs of the policy. For stabilisation to be successful, there are common characteristics that should be in place in any country:

Firstly, a credible legitimate government is needed, whose integrity transcends national borders. Concrete evidence of an improvement in governance and respect for the rule of law and property rights and commitment to institutional reform is required.

There also needs to be an acceptance by all stakeholders (including government) of the existence of an economic crisis that requires urgent attention. There must be broad consensus on crisis resolution and an acceptance by all stakeholders to bear the costs of stabilisation (temporary decline in output and hence employment).

Social pacts need to be created to negotiate the burden of adjustment across sectors and to impose a commitment to corresponding government actions. A coordinating forum between government, labour and the private sector would be required.

Bearing in mind that inflation is a monetary phenomenon, the central bank needs to be independent and not subject to political manipulation. There must be external financing support to underpin the stabilisation programme and to mitigate adverse effects. Such external support is necessary to both stabilise the currency and deal with the social dimensions of stabilisation.

Challenges to stabilisation in Zimbabwe

There are a number of challenges facing a stabilisation process in Zimbabwe. The starting point is abnormal inflation and a consolidated budget deficit that at the time of writing was in excess of 80% of GDP. As at the end of September 2008, independent inflation figures put inflation in excess of 26 000% for the month of September, with the year-on-year (YOY) figure of over a trillion percent

(1.1 trillion%) on food inflation. The YOY estimate by the end of the year will be in tens of quadrillions, even with a tapering off of the monthly inflation rate.[1]

In several respects, Zimbabwe's economic crisis is structural in nature. Land ownership was not a problem that emerged suddenly nor was the failure to create sufficient jobs to absorb school-leavers. Similarly, the fiscal balance has been a serious constraint throughout the post-independence period, while the country has lived with an underlying balance of payments problem for the past 50 years. Above all, Zimbabwe's long-run growth record is poor, so that by the turn of the century per capita incomes were lower than in 1960.

Hyperinflation has in many ways made the Zimbabwe dollar redundant. US dollarisation has increased markedly since the middle of 2008, though it is still illegal in many instances. The financial sector is under severe stress due to Reserve Bank policies aimed at extracting revenue from banks. Banks largely undertake very little financial intermediation in matching short-term lenders with longer-term borrowers.

Mining sector production has been declining steadily because of excessive taxation (including the tax imposed by surrendering requirements to the RBZ) and the prospects for new investments are clouded by uncertainties over the Indigenisation Act. Formal businesses are now simply closing operations and retrenching staff.

Furthermore, the military pervades the economy (in state institutions, parastatals and the private sector). It also plays a dominant role in the development of national policy (through its prominent role in the Joint Operations Command [JOC]) and is central to enforcing policies such as price controls.

The state is extensively involved throughout the economy through parastatals and the activities of the RBZ. Government-owned or -controlled parastatals are significant in utilities, infrastructure, mining, commerce, agriculture and finance.

The collapse of the power sector is a major obstacle to economic recovery. Many existing facilities are in need of rehabilitation. Thermal stations have difficulty accessing coal, in part due to the rail system running below 10% capacity (only eight trains a day). There is a major power deficit and load shedding is routine, constraining industry and agriculture. About 40% of power is currently imported, but the region may not be able to sustain this supply.

The agricultural sector is in a state of near collapse. Overall, export crop volumes have plummeted over the past decade to about a quarter of previous levels. Zimbabwe is facing massive and unprecedented food insecurity. The 2008 Food and Agriculture Organization of the United Nations/World Food Programme Food

and Crop Assessment showed that an estimated 5.1 million people would be food insecure by January 2009. With the exception of 1992, when there was a major drought, the 2008 crop was the worst since independence and will only meet about a third of Zimbabwe's food needs.

Outward migration has generated large volumes of remittances in cash and in kind that have been critical in maintaining many families' consumption. However, the loss of skills in the public sector (teachers, health workers, engineers, bureaucrats and managers) and the private sector have dented Zimbabwe's capacity.

Basic service provision is quickly collapsing and the ability to pay for private provision is weak. Social sector indicators are alarming. Only 5% of teachers returned to work when the new term began in October 2008, school examinations were clouded in shambles and universities have remained closed since March 2008. One in three children are not getting life-saving vaccinations for preventable diseases. The broader economic and humanitarian situation worsens Zimbabwe's ability to respond to the challenge of HIV/AIDs. Even though the HIV prevalence rate has gone down in recent years, at the time of writing 2,500 adults died of AIDS every week and 2 000 or more children were orphaned.

It is hoped that the above issues will be kept in mind by the new administration, especially if the donor community as well as private sector investors hold back for some or all of the transitional period. This point is critical since, without substantial foreign assistance, sustainable economic recovery will be impossible.

Issues for stabilisation

Sequencing of the programme

The roundtable discussion generally agreed that the sequencing of the programme is as important as its formulation. Following a decade of decline, full economic recovery with a return to sustainable, inclusive growth needs to be understood as a lengthy, three-phase process:

- Phase One – short-term economic stabilisation, lasting at least two years;

- Phase Two – institutional and structural reforms designed to create a solid platform for strong growth. Ideally, some of these reforms should be implemented – or at least initiated – during Phase One;

- Phase Three – second-generation institutional and structural reforms that are necessary to ensure that growth is both sustainable and inclusive and that Zimbabwe avoids short-lived growth spells that prove unsustainable, as has been seen in other sub-Saharan African economies. Many, perhaps most, of these second-generation reforms will have to be launched during Phase Two, but the process will be complex and the delivery period lengthy.

Short-to-medium-term stabilisation needs to be in the context of securing a platform for long-run growth. In the first ninety days of the installation of the post-crisis administration the following steps should be taken:

- The new government should increase its dialogue with key actors (both domestic and international) on possible re-engagement plans;

- The donor community should, as a matter of urgency, prepare a needs assessment and joint donor engagement strategy;

- The new government should prepare an interim budget statement, which will lay the foundations for the development of an interim Poverty Reduction Strategy Paper (PRSP). In Zimbabwe, it is generally agreed that there is sufficient material to draw up such an interim PRSP, including that from the United Nations Development Programme (UNDP), bilateral initiatives, the World Bank Multi Donor Trust Fund (MDTF), and local and regional think-tanks, businesses and non-state stakeholders.

The roundtable participants emphasised that the plan for the first 90 days should be understood as only one part of a normal short-term stabilisation programme, which should lay the foundations for the following medium to long-term economic baseline:

- Coherent, effective macroeconomic stability;

- Efficient institutional reforms and frameworks;

- Sound macroeconomic management;

- Institutional reform to build a developmental state.

These long-run development issues all point to institutional and structural reforms as well as appropriate strategies designed to restore sustainable, equitable growth and to eradicate poverty.

Proposed targets of programme implementation[2]

January – March 2009

- Firm commitment to the rule of law, respect for property rights and independence of the judiciary;
- Fiscal discipline oversight through the creation of relevant parliamentary committees;
- Commitment to and the start of dialogue with regional and international financial institutions on economic reform;
- An International Monetary Fund (IMF) visit, full information disclosure and substantive policy discussions with government;
- Announcement of a stabilisation package (fiscal & monetary).

    The early benchmarks of progress will include:

- An invitation to the IMF and Multilateral Development Banks (MDBs) for substantive policy dialogue and agreement on a monitored programme;
- The announcement of a stabilisation budget, exchange rate reforms and agreement for a stabilisation programme;
- The establishment of a track record on economic stabilisation.

April – December 2009

- Continue and consolidate the implementation of the elements of the first 90 days programme;
- Implement monetary-based stabilisation, leave exchange rate to the market, remove all exchange and trade controls;
- Firm commitment to price stability and separation of powers over fiscal policy (Minister of Finance) and monetary policy (RBZ).

January 2010 - December 2011

- Equitable, transparent and effective revenue collection;
- Institutional reform measures to be in place for building a developmental state.

    The elements of an orthodox stabilisation programme are elaborated below. They represent the best practices and generally successful episodes of stabilisation programmes. It will be up to the new government, in consultation with its key stakeholders, both domestic non-state players and international donors, to ensure the implementation of the agreed upon stabilisation package.

An overview of current proposals on short-term stabilisation in Zimbabwe

Comprehensive Economic Recovery	
Price liberalisation	• Remove price (including interest rate) controls • Announce pre-planting prices for first two agricultural seasons
Exchange rate liberalisation	• Remove exchange rate controls on current transactions and transfers • Allow exchange rate to be market-determined • Remove capital controls on private individuals • Unify the exchange rate by first establishing a single official rate that is then steadily depreciated toward market-determined levels (reference parallel market rate)
RBZ and financial sector	• Restructure the RBZ and return it to its core function of stabilising prices • Revise the RBZ Act and grant autonomy to the central bank • Recapitalise commercial banks • Restore liquidity by reducing statutory reserve requirements and restructuring the RBZ discount window • Improve the regulatory environment (e.g. review the RBZ Act 2004;create a Monetary Policy Committee) • Facilitate financial inclusiveness through easing barriers to the operations of microfinance institutions
Quasi-fiscal activities (QFAs)	• Eliminate QFAs • Consolidate existing QFAs into national budget • RBZ should not engage in QFAs
Monetary regimes	• Review options dollarisation, free banking and currency board (see Three Exchange Rate Options on page 44) • Partial dollarisation (whereby a preferred hard currency tender is allowed to co-exist with domestic currency of fixed monetary base) is viewed as the least controversial option • Recommend proactive monetary policy via indirect monetary control using a monetary based anchor • Establish and publish money supply growth targets • Curb excessive expenditure through printing of money and restore M1 ratio to M3 to normal levels of below 1:10

Fiscal policy	• Exercise fiscal restraint • Secure aid funding to supplement budgetary revenue • Introduce extra revenue measures • Conduct public expenditure review • Establish and publish fiscal rules • Develop rolling Medium Term Expenditure Frameworks (MTEFs)[3] • Conduct mid-term budgetary reviews • Carry out debt audit • Introduce budget caps for public enterprises • Strengthen public financial management systems
Countervail-ing measures	• Strengthen the Enhanced Social Protection Programme • Improve food aid distribution • Introduce labour-intensive public works • Improve emergency drugs/medical supplies • Extend the basic education assistance • Support children in need • Improve targeted direct transfers through the Basic Education Assistance Model (BEAM), disability allowances, medical treatment orders, food vouchers, etc.

Envisaged processes for engagement

It would be risky for any engagement process to ignore the existing framework of aid implementation architecture.

Even though all processes have their own strengths and weaknesses, the obvious strength of the existing framework is Zimbabwe's regional engagement, with South Africa and the rest of the Southern Africa Development Community (SADC) playing a pivotal role.

For example, within the current humanitarian environment, there are some donor coordination mechanisms and areas of limited interaction with the government. Some of the existing joint architectural groups include:

- UN/ Organisation of Economic Cooperation & Development (OECD) monthly coordination meetings;

- Imba Matombo – UN/World Bank jointly chaired meetings of donor heads/heads of missions (HOMs) and UN Country Team;

- Multi Donor Trust Fund Policy Group includes heads of aid agencies of contributing countries and the UN technical working groups which are open to all. Under World Bank leadership, the fund sponsors the preparation of shared technical analysis, a technical assistance facility and aid instruments for post change;

- Humanitarian coordination mechanisms – UN/Office for the Coordination of Humanitarian Affairs (OCHA).

At present, the only significant interaction between donors and the government is in:

- Health – HIV/AIDs and health programming;

- Social Welfare – Orphans and Vulnerable Children (OVC) and safety nets, food and humanitarian assistance;

- With the European Community (EC), Ministry of Finance – the Finance Secretary is the National Authorising Officer for European Development Fund resources;

- Ministry of Agriculture – food aid.

The expectation is that this and other processes in vogue will pave the way for full engagement of the new government and will be very important in the early stages of recovery. For example, coordination takes place around a PRSP. Government and donors should also organise themselves into sector and thematic groups so that policy dialogue can be harmonised and spending plans well coordinated at the sector level. Donors will also interface with government in a way that reflects aid modalities and financing vehicles, whether project or budget supports multi-donor or bilateral aid.

Among the major players at the outset will be key African institutions, namely:

- The African Development Bank (AfDB), which has a prominent leadership role to play in Zimbabwe's recovery, working closely with the IMF and World Bank. Although it is unlikely to be able to provide substantial new money to Zimbabwe early on, due to arrears, the success of the recovery package will depend on the reform agenda being developed by Zimbabweans with support from African institutions;

- South Africa and other SADC countries, which will also have a prominent role to play in Zimbabwe's recovery. Technical support and coordination between central banks will be important during currency reform. Regional development banks and the private sector will be significant players in the restoration of Zimbabwe's utilities and infrastructure;

- It is important to respect established streamlining between International Financial Institutions (IFIs)/Multilateral Development Banks (MDBs) e.g. the IMF's lead on macroeconomics and currency issues.

Three Exchange Rate Options

1.   Dollarisation (or Randisation). Zimbabwe already has a high, but unknown, degree of unofficial dollarisation. With the introduction of foreign currency shops, the public has been allowed to purchase goods from retailers in foreign currency. In addition to over 500 registered shops operating in foreign currency, the wider informal sector has long been transacting in foreign currency, making dollarisation (officially or unofficially) a de facto reality in Zimbabwe.

(Official or full dollarisation means a foreign currency – possibly the rand or in this case the US dollar – has exclusive, predominant status as full legal tender so that the domestic currency is phased out and replaced by the foreign currency. Countries that adopt this model can no longer have an independent monetary policy and set their own interest rates but must 'import' the monetary policy of the country whose currency is chosen).

2.   Free banking, which existed in Zimbabwe (then Southern Rhodesia) until 1940 when a currency board was established. This leaves private commercial banks to issue notes and other liabilities with minimal regulation. The banking system is unregulated; there are no reserve ratios, no legal restrictions on bank portfolios and no lender of last resort.

3.   A currency board must hold foreign reserves equal to 100% of the domestic money supply determined at a fixed exchange rate. As a result, money supply, and thereby interest rates, are determined entirely by market forces.

Steve H. Hanke, Zimbabwe: Hyperinflation to Growth. Harare: Imara Holdings, 2008

Recommendations and the way forward

In view of the above, the panel came up with the following recommendations as a way forward:

i. On the synergies between politics and economics, the panel agreed that a good and acceptable political settlement is a precondition for embarking on a level-headed economic stabilisation programme to match the mandate of the economic challenge.

ii. To build confidence, it is also critically important to have a strong mandate from government. A strong and organised government is needed to face the 'shock therapy' that often accompanies stabilisation and it must be able to devise and implement robust countervailing measures to cushion people from hard times. However, without the support of all stakeholders, especially the donor community, the envisaged stabilisation programme cannot succeed.

iii. It was agreed that a strong and acceptable government is needed to engage the donor community in accordance with the latest aid architecture, where both the donors and the Zimbabwean government establish reciprocal accountability based on a new set of values and compliance with new procedures. These include:

- Mutual accountability;
- Principles of donor harmonisation and alignment with country systems;
- New aid instruments, including sector-wide approaches and budget support;
- Support for the development of a PRSP;
- Increased transparency and involvement of non-governmental actors in the development of strategies.

iv. It is envisaged that the new government will seize the opportunity to take advantage of these advances in donor behaviour early on. Ideally, this will start with high-level dialogue involving the Prime Minister's office and the Minister of Finance representing the government on the one hand, and on the other the donors represented by the Multilateral Finance Institutions (MFIs): the AfDB, the World Bank, major African finance institutions, e.g. the Development Bank of Southern Africa (DBSA), the UN and the OECD.

v. A key component to the reconstruction and management of the stabilisation programme would be the creation of a 'transitional economic advisory council', which is provided for in the Global Political Agreement (GPA). The advisory council would give support to the government in the form of advice from different sector specialists and from local, regional and international players. This body could then critique advice from groups such as the IMF and World Bank. As an independent advisory body, this council should cancel out political rivalry around the advice given to government.

Eric Miller / Independent Contributors / africanpictures.net

vi. The resuscitation and revamping of institutions will be critical as many of these have been politicised, with institutional interference by politicians since the deepening of the crisis in 1997. Such institutional re-engineering should involve setting out clear and separate mandates for the Ministry of Finance in fiscal policy and that of the Reserve Bank in the area of monetary policies and price stabilisation.

vii. Policy consistency and sequencing of policies will be crucial in the new Zimbabwe so that policy credibility is maintained.

viii. Buy-in from all stakeholders, from domestic non-state stakeholders (business, labour, civic society) to the international community, will be essential.

ix. There will be a need to build capacity in the interim government to enable it to deliver and follow its new mandates.

x. In the vital sphere of land policy, the new government must spearhead policies that address both multiple land ownership and production bottlenecks on farms. It remains unclear who owns what land and how much of the land is now underutilised. A Land Commission will be needed to ensure that no single person has more than one farm. This will be addressed by the enactment of a Land Audit, as stipulated in the GPA.

xi.   The new government will immediately have to deal with the problem of the near total collapse of the domestic currency, which has effectively paved the way for the dollarisation of the economy.

Endnotes

1   This paper was written soon after the September 2008 inflation figures were released. Zimbabwe's rampant inflation has meant that this figure changes often, though recent 'dollarisation' has led to less accurate reflections of Zimbabwe dollar inflation.

2   These targets were drawn up soon after the September 2008 agreement was signed in Zimbabwe between Zanu PF and the two MDCs. Changing circumstances have made the target dates inappropriate but they remain a guideline for time-frames in future economic stabilisation planning.

3   The Medium Term Expenditure Frameworks (MDTFs) have now become the conventional three years planning horizon for yearly and medium-term plans mainly used in national programmes and coordination with international donors.

Key Issues for Security Sector Reform in Zimbabwe

By Martin Rupiya

National Security Advisor in the office of the Prime
Minister (formerly Director of Research, Africa,
Cranfield University)

Introduction

As part of a States in Transition Observatory (SITO) project, with a focus on identifying appropriate policy options for peace and security as key elements of sustainable democracy in Zimbabwe, an initiative was launched to examine the role of the security sector. Military, intelligence, police and paramilitary elements have effectively negated ordinary instruments of political transition, such as the electoral process, and other civil structures, such as the courts, through which citizens and political parties can challenge political authority. These democratic mechanisms have been set aside in an environment that has abandoned the rule of law while presenting little evidence of democratic stability. The suffering of ordinary people has become acute. The crisis has shown, and continues to demonstrate, that the use and abuse of the military (security sector) as a policy response to governance challenges has assumed pre-eminence and therefore needs to be studied if appropriate action to reverse this militarisation is to be taken in future.

This report is a summary of a roundtable discussion held in November 2008. The discussion was held under Chatham House rules to encourage open engagement by academics and practitioners, which would be non-attributable. International security experts, regional security practitioners, interested non-gov-ernmental organisations (NGOs), academics and other policy and practitioner stakeholders, including representatives on defence and security issues from the political parties, were invited to participate in the meeting. All parties responded except Zanu PF. Each of the representative delegations had an opportunity to present their own point of view on a) how they perceive the security rector reform (SSR) challenges, b) how they propose to address them, and c) what role they envisage playing if a comprehensive SSR process is launched?

Aims of the dialogue

The roundtable discussion sought to:

- Develop an understanding of the motivations that drove the changes in security policy, role and function as well as the composition of the Zimbabwean security sector after June 2000.

- Attempt to put forward appropriate policy options that contribute towards relo-cating the sector in a functioning democracy whilst restoring the ruptured civil military relations in Zimbabwe. There are regional precedents to this. Lessons can be learnt from the Tanzanian recommendations contained in the Nyalali

Commission that effectively sought to separate the party from the state, including the control of the armed forces. In the latter institution, the process also sought to remove the commissariat structure located in the president's office.

- Identify which arms of the security sector should receive turnaround attention and why? Current anecdotal evidence suggests attention be given to policing issues but the rationale for this still needs to be interrogated.

- Finally, develop specific options within the Security Sector Reform (SSR) process that relate to the broader poverty reduction, stability and development agenda of the new state, as defined by the United Nations:

  SSR processes are about assisting national authorities in restoring and reforming the security sector for purposes of peace, security, poverty reduction, economic and social development, restoring human rights, rule of law and democratization.[1]

Contextualisation

One of the unique features of the political crisis in Zimbabwe is the militarisation of politics against the background of a redefined role and function for the security sector and the executive (dominated by the military and hence hereafter simply referred to as the military). This can be referred to as the politicisation of the military. This development occurred in the context of, in retrospect, a narrowly redefined national security strategy after the June 2000 elections.

Comments by the military on the eve of that election, through its then spokesperson Major Chancellor Diye, asserted its apolitical nature and readiness to recognise the outcome of that political process and preserve its independence. However, soon after the poll, there appears to have been direct intervention by the executive, which succeeded in changing the security sector's position of non-interference in a context of declining mass popularity of the ruling party, Zanu PF. Furthermore, the country and ruling party were then preparing for the forthcoming presidential elections scheduled for March 2002.

Based on this redefined national security strategy, the military changed its tune on 9 January 2002. All the service chiefs – the Chief of Defence Staff and commanders of the army, air force, intelligence, police, prison service and national parks – appeared on national television and declared that they would not salute or recognise any leader who did not have 'liberation credentials'. This was in clear violation of the country's constitution, which allowed the registration of all citizens as candidates. In addition, from that moment onwards, the security sector in Zimbabwe, led by the military, has been at the forefront of politics in support of Zanu PF.

The security sector in Zimbabwe is represented by the following: the intelligence services, the army, police, prisons, war veterans, national service, party militia and parts of the civil service involved in the decision-making, financing and management of this sector. A trend has emerged in the internal reform of the security sector in Zimbabwe adopted by the executive: first there was a change in policy on what constitutes loyal forces. Second, at least in the earlier phases, there were clear cases in which individuals perceived as less loyal were removed. Third, new units were formed, sometimes outside the formal control of the military. All this occurred in an environment of impunity and disregard for the rule of law. Currently, the military has organised and deployed itself as the Joint Operational Command (JOC), a structure that is a throwback to the defence mechanism of the Rhodesian liberation war and that operates in an illegitimate political context.

Security Sector Reform (SSR)

Before analysing the subjective Zimbabwean challenges to the reform of the security sector, there is a need to briefly restate what this process is normatively understood to entail. SSR is actually an old notion that should, ideally, take place continuously within states as the military is reformed for different political, economic and geo-strategic reasons, such as the democratisation process identified in Samuel Huntington's *Third Wave of Democratization*. The purpose of SSR is to create institutions that are responsible for policy formulation and implementation of activities that comprehensively address the security interests of a state and its society.

One can ask, does Africa have apolitical security forces or militaries? According to writers on the question of military withdrawal from politics as the continent marched towards multi-party democracy, there is no military that can be cited as truly non-partisan. However, to the extent that as an institution each supports and reinforces the pillars of the state, outside the actual political party poll hustings, the notion of an apolitical military is relevant. In cases where the military takes an active political role designed to bring about the electoral victory of a particular party against another, and where the military may even define the country's national security and economic policies, then the military as an institution is seen to have lost its preferred apolitical nature.

This was evident in the Tanzanian multiparty review process during the 1990s. The late Justice Francis Nyalali in his report (hereafter simply referred to as the Nyalali Commission) recommended reform of the highly politicised and integrated military, the Tanzanian Peoples Defence Force (TPDF). The re-emergence of SSR on the African continent is associated with events in the 1990s when international donors linked SSR to political deregulation and support conditionalities. As a result, the idea has drawn more critics and resistance than would have been the case otherwise.

SSR is today guided by new notions of security included in policies such as the African Union's (AU's) Common African Defence and Security Policy (CADSP) that has recognised the centrality of state security while paying equal attention to notions of human security as articulated by the United Nations Development Programme (UNDP) in 1994. It is, in fact, a political process concerned with changing power relations in the field of security policy, management and institutional support structures. Conducted in a post-conflict situation, SSR has winners and losers and therefore some who welcome the process and others who resist it. Furthermore, SSR generally includes, either in its genesis or as challenges to its implementation, the realities of Disarmament, Demobilisation and Reintegration (DDR).

Key SSR issues

While this process is not prescriptive we must emerge from the discussions with concrete policy options to be fed into the arena of policy in the event that the Global Political Agreement is implemented. To this end, the following points were identified as key issues for special attention during the dialogue:

Firstly, what sort of national security strategy should form the basis of responding to the new political dispensation? This refers not only to the governance component, concerned with policy formulation and implementing agencies, but also to identifying the preferred actors. Precedents include the transformation in

Lori Waselchuk / South Photographs / africanpictures.net

South Africa after 1994 as well as the earlier events in Malawi after the departure of former president Hastings Banda. In both cases, reform of the national security strategy included constitutional review of the Defence and Police Acts as part of the wider consultative renewal. While this can restore the civil-military relations balance and give legitimacy to the new institutions, it can also provide clear demarcation of when and where the military may be used in response to both internal and external security situations.

Secondly, what is the composition of the security sector in the country and

does this engender confidence and legitimacy among the local community and external stakeholders? What changes have occurred in the sector since June 2000 and have these complemented or detracted from the national security plan under the Coalition Agreement of 1980? To this end, it is important to examine the nature of recruitment for national service in August 2002 and the extent to which the same practice should be used in future.

Thirdly, what is the parliamentary oversight role within the new state? This is important given the gradual marginalisation of observations made, for example, by Lieutenant Colonel (ret.) Shumba and MP Mrs Gladys Hokoyo as leading members of the parliamentary defence and security committee whose findings may prove useful, though at the time they were simply ignored. Furthermore, parliament ordinarily authorises the decisions by the executive, approves the appointment of senior officers, and represents the authority that declares war, raises armies, approves funds and creates instruments regulating the conditions of service and other related interactions with foreign or neighbouring state militaries. What roles have been stripped from parliament in Zimbabwe? How can these be restored and strengthened?

Fourthly, is there a role for civil society organisations, including media and policy research institutes, specialising in issues of peace and security within the SSR process? Where these have been deliberately dispersed, as is the evidence from the Southern African Political Economy Series (SAPES), what recommendations can be made for the SSR process to include independent bodies with a mandate to monitor and evaluate progress in the new era?

What needs to be done in terms of legal and institutional civic education to restore credibility to the police and establish a new approach to prisons in the country? Stated differently, is there a correctional or punishment-based prison system? Further, has gender been a dimension that requires attention in the make-up of the new force in the future?

What have been the levels of military expenditure since June 2000? Has this been a priority in relation to other sectors and can this be examined with a view to creating institutions that are appropriate, affordable and adequate? Is there value in rethinking former Minister Bernard Chidzero's location of military camps in the remote rural areas as economic agents or have these camps been compromised?

What are the key challenges to repairing regional security arrangements that have been disrupted by the protracted crisis in Zimbabwe? This may include the repositioning of the Regional Peacekeeping and Training Centre based at King George the 6th Barracks (KG VI). The second issue at a regional level is the extent to which the new national security strategy contains elements of common and collaborative security, directly addressing the question of the supremacy of the sovereign state.

What is the current security decision-making process that, from the outside at least, appears dominated by ruling party, Central Committee and Politburo structures rather than state organs? Is there a role for military professionalism in the new era and if this is the case, how can this be effected? To this end, military leadership is key to nuanced professionalism. What would be the recommended background, education, ethnic and regional balance for the new officer corps?

Finally, what elements of the security sector can provide what is known as 'low-hanging-fruit' to bring about maximum effect from a comprehensive process? In other words, would attention to reforming the police be the correct priority?

In Zimbabwe, the transformation of the security sector to serve a political purpose for a party that has been unable to draw popular support has left the country divided and polarised. Not only has this undermined the previous balance in civil-military relations but it has also had serious implications for legitimacy and regional integration, as well as a negative budgetary impact. If this argument is correct, then the country represents a clear case study for root and branch SSR in the event that there is a political agreement in the near future.

Dialogue

The procedure followed at the roundtable discussion was to offer the political parties the floor, followed by (Southern African) regional defence and security practitioners, regional players, academics and other interested parties. Because this was a small and select group, everyone present had the opportunity to say something. What follows below is not a verbatim report of the proceedings but rather a summarised version highlighting significant points, decisions and recommendations that emerged from the discussion.

The core Zimbabwean security forces under consideration are composed of approximately 60 000 mainly men and a few women organised as the army (35 000), police (30 000), the air force (5 000) and the Central Intelligence Organisation (CIO). On paper, the CIO is composed of only 3 000 people but in practice the numbers are estimated to be closer to 15 000. There are also quasi-civilian and party establishments, difficult to quantify in numbers, working with the security sector, such as the national service, party militia and war veterans. Where in the past the sector had strong regional security links, these have recently shrunk and the military is shunned in open engagement with other regional security sector institutions that are uncomfortable with the overt political role adopted by the Zimbabwean military. The last major political involvement of the military occurred between 29th March and 27th June 2008. During this period, the military spread themselves countrywide, addressed rallies and argued for the re-election of Zanu PF and its candidates.

The house was informed that the CIO was the most feared structure, operating openly as the vanguard of Zanu PF and responsible for the day-to-day operations of the ruling party. This was organised around the military intelligence structure, the Police Internal Security Intelligence (PISI), the Zanu PF intelligence structure under Minister Nicholas Goche but operating as indivisible from the formal CIO, a presidential intelligence arm and an air force intelligence component. Secondly, it emerged that the different forces of the police, army, prisons and national service do not have a cohesive central structure; with some being favoured above others. The military, for example, is better remunerated than the police. For the state, establishing these different and competing sources of intelligence has created a sense of uncertainty within the ranks. As a result, one can still ask, 'who-guards-the-guards?'

Key outcomes

The meeting agreed that the following are the core areas that need to be addressed in an SSR process in Zimbabwe.

1. Reconsider the unsustainable number of the current combined forces. This will involve the DDR into society of thousands of soldiers. However, the country currently neither has the political will nor the resources to do this.
2. Seek to identify and engage with 'low-hanging-fruit' which are units or elements, such as the police, likely to offer maximum benefit with minimum cost implications in reform. This would be in the context of using this as a vanguard for more sustained, comprehensive SSR.
3. Revisit the role of parliament and its oversight over allocation of resources, mediation between the executive and the security sector, and monitoring of the extent to which the security sector operates under the provisions of the constitution.
4. Investigate and determine the levels of security sector expenditure for the purpose of linking future allocations to wider national economic recovery.
5. Reconsider the question of re-professionalisation in light of the politicisation that has created a gap between society and the security institutions. In doing this, it was suggested that an appropriate National Defence Act emerge from a National Security Strategy Review (NSSR) that draws its inspiration from a broader constitutional review process.
6. It also emerged that the Zimbabwean forces have lost the confidence and respect of regional security structures, denting the role that the Regional Peacekeeping Training Centre (RPTC) had been set up to play.

Entry points identified

First, concerted contact must be made with parliamentarians who are ready and willing to play a role in addressing the role and function of the security sector. It was revealed that there was cross-party consensus on this issue in parliament, which included Zanu PF parliamentarians, although recently it appears Zanu PF MPs have been ordered not to interact with others on issues related to the security sector.

Second, it emerged that the security sector is divided and a baseline study should be conducted to determine precisely which sectors provide opportunities for engagement. Such a study would identify potential openings for and catalysts in a reform process.

Third, a comprehensive SSR process would need to factor in mechanisms designed to revive the role of a cowed and abused civil society community. Previously, civil society was engaged in research and commentary on peace and security issues. The expectation is that not only would this restore vibrant organizations, such as SAPES, but it would also reform private media houses now directly owned by the CIO and other state security sector organisations.

Fourth, the debate suggested that in the future a focus on who and what institutions represent the security sector needed to be seriously considered as the current institutions had allowed themselves to be appropriated in a partisan agenda at the expense of their national mandate.

Fifth, the question of perceived levels of expenditure and prioritisation of the security question over and above other economic and social demands needed to be raised as well as an assessment of security expenditure in relation to broader national security concerns.

Sixth, restoring damaged regional security cooperation emerged as an urgent issue to be addressed by actors, including those who sit on the parliamentary defence and security committee.

Seventh, the composition of a reformed security sector needs to respond to gender, racial, regional and ethnic dimensions in terms of the equitable sharing of posts and responsibility as a necessary foundation for future recovery and stability.

Finally, there is a need to review the current security policy as well as the decision-making process. State security policy was perceived to have been combined with the personal security of the political elite and ruling party rather than more holistic conceptions of national security. In addition, decisions about security matters – in particular, defining what constitutes a national threat have been compromised by personal and partisan positions and perceptions. As a result, there needs to be a review of the constitutionally mandated functions of government, the civil service and the executive branch. Furthermore, the role perceived to be played by certain key party structures at present illustrates that security sector policy remains the preserve of the politburo, central committee and related party channels rather than being subject to oversight by the national government.

Conclusion

The Zimbabwe crisis is characterised by significant military involvement in politics and this has militarised the political context. The security sector in Zimbabwe has been transformed. It has become divisive and, as a result, certain actors treat particular units with preference, which has created tensions. In the event of a political solution to the current crisis, the security sector will require robust intervention. The cost of expenditure on maintaining and sustaining the security sector needs to be quantified. It is unsustainable and has come at the expense of other demands related to social welfare, industry and investment.

Parliament, in particular, has had its oversight of the security sector reduced. This should be the first important area for engagement if future progress is to be made.

Finally, although Zanu PF MPs and representatives did not attend the dialogue, their deliberations with their colleagues in parliament suggest that they are aware of the military challenge, especially the cost to the fiscus, and are awaiting an appropriate moment to engage with the issue of SSR.

Endnote

1   See 'Preface' in Heiner Hanggi & Vincencza Scherer (Eds) Security Sector Reform and UN Integrated Missions: Experience from Burundi, the Democratic Republic of Congo, Haiti and Kosovo Geneva Centre for the Democratic Control of Armed forces (DCAF), 2008.

Acronyms

AfDB	African Development Bank
AU	African Union
BEAM	Basic Education Assistance Model
EC	European Community
CADSP	Common African Defence and Security Policy
CCJP	Catholic Commission for Justice and Peace
CIO	Central Intelligence Organisation
DDR	Disarmament, Demobilisation and Reintegration
FAO/WFP	Food and Agricultural Organisation/World Food Programme
GPA	Global Political Agreement
HOM	Head of Missions
IFI	International Financial Institution
IMF	International Monetary Fund
JOMIC	Joint Monitoring and Implementation Committee
JOC	Joint Operations Command
LRF	Legal Resources Foundation
MDB	Multilateral Development Bank
MDC	Movement for Democratic Change
MDTF	Multi Donor Trust Fund
MOU	Memorandum of Understanding
MTEF	Medium Term Expenditure Framework
NCA	National Constitutional Assembly
NSSR	National Security Strategy Review
OVC	Orphans and Vulnerable Children
PISI	Police Internal Security Intelligence
PRSP	Poverty Reduction Strategy Paper
QFA	Quasi Fiscal Activity
RBZ	Reserve Bank of Zimbabwe
RTGS	Real Team Gross Settlement
RPTC	Regional Peacekeeping Training Centre
SADC	Southern African Development Community
SAPES	Southern African Political Economy Series
TRC	Truth and Reconciliation Commission
UNDP	United Nations Development Programme
OCHA	Office for the Coordination of Humanitarian Affairs
OECD	Organisation of Economic Cooperation & Development
SITO	States in Transition Observatory
SSR	Security Sector Reform
UN	United Nations
WB	World Bank
YOY	Year-on-Year
ZANU PF	Zimbabwe African National Union – Patriotic Front
ZCTU	Zimbabwean Congress of Trades Unions